THE POCKET GUIDE TO ACTION

THE POCKET GUIDE TO ACTION

116 Meditations on the Art of Doing

KYLE ESCHENROEDER

First Printing, 2016
ISBN 978-0-9891903-7-4
Published by Semper Virilis Publishing
www.artofmanliness.com

ACKNOWLEDGEMENTS

The following people put a lot of time and energy into making this book better than I ever could have on my own, thank you: Kate McKay, Jeremy Anderberg, Brett McKay, Stephanie Ziajka, Brook Eschenroeder, Jesse Eschenroeder, Mansal Denton, Ludvig Sunström, Charlie Diaz, and Morgan Miller.

INTRODUCTION

"Our grand business is not to see what lies dimly
at a distance, but to do what lies clearly at hand."

■ THOMAS CARLYLE ■

> *"Precept is a very good thing, but to my thinking an ounce of practical energy is worth any amount of precept without action."*
>
> ■ **THEODORE ROOSEVELT** ■

THERE'S A KIND of listless, restless, low-grade anxiety permeating our society today. There are many causes from a culture-wide perspective: over-stimulation, declining levels of trust in those around us and our institutions, the displacement of human workers with machines at increasing speeds, lack of central values, proliferating lifestyle options (and social media to toggle through them all), collapsing narratives, and many, many more.

It seems impossible to have a worthwhile idea that others haven't had already. It seems impossible to say something that hasn't been said. It seems impossible to have a strong opinion on things that matter. It seems impossible to decide on which course to take. It seems impossible to find purpose—to find meaningful work and meaningful relationships. So we focus on TV shows and sporting events. (Or we turn our politics into something as trivial.)

The way out of this feeling of confusion and meaninglessness on a societal level is difficult. It involves shifts in our economics, collective narratives, and politics that are nearly impossible to envision, much less implement.

Luckily for us, individuals have a much simpler solution: *action.*

We've lost sight of what it means to take action. Not to mention what it means to take *right* action.

Taking action is not flailing around purposelessly or keeping yourself busy while avoiding the real problem.

What it *is*...well, that's what the rest of this book will explore.

To begin reorienting to a life of action requires something which at first appears to be non-action: meditations. We have to contemplate what action is and understand how it plays out in our lives.

We have to learn not only its more direct, "blunt force" expressions with which we're most familiar, but also the subtleties of action: imagination, reflection, and waiting can all be some of its most powerful forms. At the same time, we can appear to be doing all sorts of things externally without actually taking a meaningful action. As Thoreau asked, "It is not enough to be industrious; so are the ants. *What are you industrious about?*"

Action is the surest path not only to reaching goals, but to finding the kind of meaning and purpose we desire. It is a kind of back door to the promises of so many philosophies and religions. When we are action-oriented, we forget to notice the missing pieces of our modern world: anomie fades away, change doesn't seem so wildly fast, the news becomes white noise.

I wrote these meditations on action for myself a couple years ago because I needed them. When I wrote them I was feeling stuck. Between projects, between relationships, between exercise regimens—nothing seemed worthwhile. I was facing a crippling existential crisis. The only relief came when I lowered my expectations for my abstract mind and focused on what was actually going on. This didn't always mean doing different things (although often it did); it meant *being* in a more active way.

I have visited this book regularly since then to get recentered and reinvigorated—it works every time. I hope it will have the same effect on you.

If you're experiencing crippling paralysis or acutely anxious restlessness, try reading the book all the way through to jumpstart movement with a new mindset and in a new direction.

Or carry this pocket-sized book wherever you go, and open it up whenever you have a spare minute and need a kick in the pants. The passages are short and designed to spur you to powerful action.

A NOTE TO THE READER: DEFINING ABSTRACTION AND ACTION

A quick note on words before we begin. I'll use "abstraction" primarily to discuss "over abstraction." Abstraction is useful, but, as you will see, it's less useful than it seems.

Abstraction is a type of thinking, the type that considers ideas more important than events.

"Action" is used here synonymously with "right action."

Right actions are bold and deliberate. They carry the potential for flow and mindfulness. Right actions are virtuous. They bring us closer to understanding reality while bringing our imaginations to life.

Action is endlessly searching for the right lifehack to finally make you productive; right action is getting to work. Action is eating a Twinkie; right action is eating chicken breasts and broccoli. Action is punching someone because they root for a different sports team; right action is punching someone who's beating up someone weaker.

Right actions aren't usually grand. They can be small. Brushing your teeth is an action. Brushing your teeth mindfully is right action.

PART I:
PHILOSOPHY AS ACTION

"The cucumber is bitter? Then throw it out. There are brambles in the path? Then go around. That's all you need to know."

■ MARCUS AURELIUS ■

HOW TO LIVE?

Action focuses this philosophical question into practice by transforming abstract reasoning into concrete reality.

Worthwhile philosophers are connected to reality.

Theories do no good unless they can reliably guide action—in our thinking and our physical actions.

Twenty minutes of meditation will show you what hours of reading the *Bhagavad Gita* never could. The concept of virtue is useless unless it drives your behavior.

You can never know if a theory is practical until you put it into action.

When you take a step forward you can truly *grok* a theory. You can *feel* what was being talked about.

And then you know whether or not the idea works for you. In other words, you now understand the only thing that matters.

> *"To be a philosopher is not merely to have subtle thoughts, nor even to found a school...it is to solve some of the problems of life, not only theoretically, but practically."*
>
> ■ **HENRY DAVID THOREAU** ■

INACTION IS EXPENSIVE

If we try and fail, we see the cost. The number of hours and dollars spent on the project. We feel the pain when it doesn't work. The embarrassment is acute.

This makes inaction tempting.

We don't consider refusing to choose as a choice. We think we're safe if we don't expose ourselves to failure. We don't appreciate the consequences of inaction because they are slow, chronic, and non-obvious. That's what makes them dangerous.

You don't get to escape pain.

The pain that comes with action is acute, scars you, and makes you grow.

The pain that comes from inaction is low-grade, softens you, and decays your soul.

YOU ARE NOT "WAITING TO LIVE"...

You are waiting to act.

That stagnation, low-grade frustration, and perpetual exhaustion comes from your refusal to act.

The reason you don't feel alive is because you've worn yourself out thinking about things instead of actually *doing* them. You haven't moved because your habit is to flinch away from action.

You unconsciously refuse to see the falsity in your old beliefs, your old fears, and your old habits.

Action means pushing into a new way of living that you have not imagined before. It means pushing through what you're scared of into what you couldn't even think to be scared of.

It means pushing through all that, seeing that it wasn't as bad as you thought, then doing it again.

Committing to action doesn't end once you get somewhere. It means you never stop pushing.

WHAT IS UP TO US ISN'T UP TO US

We can head in a certain direction. We can avoid the paths we know are bad. We can adopt a philosophy for living.

We cannot know what will happen. We cannot live in (or predict) the future. We cannot choose the choices we're faced with

We can't tame Fate. We can't predict the future.

All we can know is how we will act when the rubber meets the road.

We can train ourselves to be more prepared.

We can't change what's happened. Only what we do now.

ACTING IS DIRTY

Creation is inherently messy. The Big Bang created everything we know in a massive explosion. You were born into this world bloody while your mother endured the worst pain of her life.

Modern movies, video games, and novels generally follow a clean narrative. We might not know exactly what will happen, but we know the general contours. The hero will be challenged, he will either be victorious or temporarily beaten. Either way he'll be redeemed by the end of the story. Life doesn't offer this guarantee.

Honest action won't take you on a straight path. It may not make sense to you or those around you at first.

Instead, it will straighten your posture on any path you're on. You won't fear what others fear. You won't regret what the others will.

You'll have scars and remember the lessons they taught you. Others will be fragile because while they kept their training wheels on you let yourself fall down, endure the pain, and do it again.

"*If our young men miscarry in their first enterprises, they lose all heart. If the young merchant fails, men say he is ruined. If the finest genius studies at one of our colleges, and is not installed in an office within one year afterwards in the cities or suburbs of Boston or New York, it seems to his friends and to himself that he is right in being disheartened, and in complaining the rest of his life. A sturdy lad from New Hampshire or Vermont, who in turn tries all the professions, who teams it, farms it, peddles, keeps a school, preaches, edits a newspaper, goes to Congress, buys a township, and so forth, in successive years, and always, like a cat, falls on his feet, is worth a hundred of these city dolls. He walks abreast with his days, and feels no shame in not 'studying a profession,' for he does not postpone his life, but lives already. He has not one chance, but a hundred chances.*"

■ **RALPH WALDO EMERSON** ■
SELF-RELIANCE

BOOKS ABOUT HEAVEN

Steven Pressfield relates a *New Yorker* cartoon in his (short) book *Do the Work*: "A perplexed person stands before two doors. One door says HEAVEN. The other says BOOKS ABOUT HEAVEN."

He's perplexed. He's *considering* the book over the actual experience. It's funny because it's absurd...and because we know we'd have the same consideration.

Why would we deny ourselves direct experience?

Action is going to Heaven. Abstraction is reading about going to Heaven.

(Reading a book *can* be Heaven when it's a primary activity.)

"SPARTANS DO NOT ASK HOW MANY ARE THE ENEMY..."

> *"...but where are they."*
>
> ■ PLUTARCH, *SAYINGS OF THE SPARTANS* ■

The Spartans knew they would meet the enemy and fight with courage. They didn't ask for unnecessary information.

You don't need to either.

Gather the minimum information you need to begin.

Then, before you think you're ready, begin.

This will provide you more useful information than any amount of abstract research ever could.

PART II:
LOOKING AT ACTION

"*To will and not to do when there is opportunity is in reality not to will; and to love what is good and not to do it, when it is possible, is in reality not to love it.*"

■ **EMANUEL SWEDENBORG** ■

MOTIVATION FOLLOWS ACTION

Our fatal mistake is waiting to be motivated before we take action.

Action motivates.

I don't feel like working out until I get my blood flowing. I'm too tired to have sex until we've begun. I don't want to go to the party until I'm there.

Motivation will follow if you have the balls to go without them.

ACT TO BECOME

How you perceive the world changes the way you act in it. This is the basis of a thousand psychology books. Neuro-plasticity, the placebo effect, neuro-linguistic programming, and countless other findings show us that our internal world shapes our external world. This is true, and, like all good truths, so is its opposite:

Your internal world is changed by the external world.

Taking action out there shapes your "in here."

You don't need to convince yourself you are a healthy eater to eat well.

You don't need to convince yourself you are a playboy in order to ask that girl out.

You don't need to convince yourself you are a filmmaker in order to shoot a film.

Stop treating perceptions as primary. Let labels conform to your actions.

Instead of waiting to feel like working towards who you'd like to be, act in line with that desire, and the feelings will follow.

Act to become.

EXPERIENCE IS THE BEST TEACHER

When Mother told you the fire would be painful, did you believe her? Did you become adept at basic arithmetic when your teacher gave the lesson or after hours of practice? Did talking about the birds and the bees save you from fumbling around awkwardly?

It's better if we can avoid mistakes than make them all on our own. It's better if we can learn not to touch the fire by the examples of others.

Sometimes we can't though. A lot of times. Sometimes, in fact, it's better that we don't.

THE MOST VALUABLE RESOURCE

If you want to make something (a movie, book, business, painting, website), make it. Technology is cheap.

If you don't, chances are you were more attracted to the title than the activity.

The scarcity in our world is in initiative, not the resources to produce.

A GOOD FUTURE DOES NOT DEPEND ON A PERFECT VISUALIZATION

It depends on long strings of right actions.

Some scientists and philosophers say we don't know anything for sure. Every scientific "law" is just waiting to be disproved.

If we can't be sure of gravity (and Einstein wasn't), then why do we feel the need to infuse our predictions of the future with such faith?

(The only thing I can predict with any certainty is how I will act, and that is only possible if I practice right action daily.)

You don't know where you'll be in a year for sure, but you can push in a certain direction.

You may not know what you want to do with your life. You may be somewhat certain you want to be healthy, though. Nobody has ever regretted eating well and exercising. Your future is almost guaranteed to be better if you do those things.

It doesn't guarantee you health (you may break your back or get cancer) or happiness, but it will give you a much better chance at both.

"ANYTHING CAN WORK."

Alfonso Cuaron, director of *Gravity*, said that at a round-table discussion with David O. Russell, Steve McQueen, and Ben Stiller. The directors were discussing methods and techniques; you could see Cuaron getting frustrated.

As they were attempting to grasp at what makes a great director great, Alfonso understood that there *is no answer.*

Sure, they all try really hard. Beyond that there is no formula.

Cuaron understood that every situation is different. It's less about rules and more about posture. You can't make *2001: A Space Odyssey* twice, but you *can* make something as great.

Lean into the thing and see what works for this specific instance. What worked last time may not work this time.

As you test, follow what works. It may not agree with accepted wisdom. It might even be the opposite of what you were told to expect. Follow what is working *now.*

ACTION IS WILD

Zoo animals get depressed.

A caged lion has a longer life expectancy, more wealth, and a more predictable career than his wild counterpart.

Yet his mind is dull because there is no danger. He moves slowly because he is no longer hungry.

We aimed at comfort for ourselves and, when we got it, gave it to wild animals.

It's not working out for either party. What looks comfortable, isn't.

COMFORT

The best life isn't the most comfortable one. Yet that's where our goals tend to lie.

Comfort causes depression and anxiety.

Action throws us into discomfort. It makes us exert effort and try out the unknown.

Consistent action pushes you into a life where you don't have to borrow from the Kardashian's drama, where the question of meaning in life is answered by effort, where time works for us instead of against us.

All you have to do is push past the momentary flinch—the acute discomfort you feel when you grow.

ACTION IS THE PATH

Action appears to reveal paths. On closer inspection, though, it is the path.

Action is faith in the present moment.

Action allows us to see beyond what we could see standing still.

Action pulls the internal and external worlds into harmony. Constant feedback is required to make sense of the deluge of information coming at us. This middle (internal-external) path does not reject reality, it accepts it and sees how malleable it is. The middle path does not fear the present—it understands impermanence. The middle path does not judge, it knows.

THE MAP IS NOT THE TERRITORY

We need maps to understand where to go next. We need a wider perspective. The more information on a map, though, the *less* it shows.

A map of your neighborhood provides much different information than a globe.

A walk down your street provides a much different experience than looking at the street on a map.

Looking at the map can help you plot a course. It can help you know what streets to expect. That's it, though.

It doesn't tell you anything about the houses, trees, or wild cats you will pass. It doesn't tell you about the kids who are going to sell you lemonade. It can't know that your future lover lives in the house with the bird feeder.

You've got to go on the walk to find these things.

A map is helpful; awareness is imperative.

ACTION IS CHANGE

My great-grandfather gave me this advice after I graduated high school: "Don't change." He wasn't kidding.

Talk about setting a kid up for failure.

That remark changed me. It was the first time I considered staying still as a goal.

It's scary.

Partly because you're aiming away from anything new, partly because it's impossible.

FAILING IN ACTION

When you fail while acting it isn't a failure at all. It's process. You can't escape the benefits: experience, strength, knowledge, relationships, etc. This kind of failure creates new options, new potentials.

The failure of inaction is much more insidious. It isn't immediately as painful, and so it is much more seductive. The downside is much more serious: you get none of the benefits of action, and you are faced with knowing that you are a coward—that you never even tried.

Bold action may always scare you, as it should, but never as much as the alternative: timidity. Inaction is the cancer that will eat away at your soul until it is gone. That's scarier than anything.

ACTION IS REVOLUTIONARY

Nearly all the things that shake the world come out of nowhere. A boring (looking) scientist or businessman hard at work changes things far more than someone sitting around with a mission statement and a proclamation to change the world.

While 100 "entrepreneurs" online are busy updating their profiles and posting links to business-y articles on their Facebook page, there is one entrepreneur (without a Facebook page) with his head down getting work done.

You can spend your time arguing about national politics or getting involved in your local government. One pleases the ego, the other makes a difference.

Action looks boring. It's often not loud while it's happening. But the result is frequently revolutionary.

ACTION IS UNGRASPABLE

We won't be able to understand all our actions all the way, right away. Sometimes we have to do things and we don't know why until years later. We're sitting having a beer with an old friend and in the middle of the conversation we get hit with it. *So that's why I had to do that.*

Action takes faith. That it will make sense later. That the lessons you learned here matter. We are conscious of very little of what we understand.

Do you think, *"I better not touch the stove"* when you know it's hot? No. You understand it so thoroughly that you don't require an explanation. Lessons learned through action have this kind of depth.

No human can explain his or her life completely. Yet we go to great lengths to do just that.

The most liberating response to, "Why did you do that?"

Because I had to.

YOU'VE ALREADY DECIDED

Neuroscientists have shown that we decide before we're conscious of making the decision. We have decided to eat the last bite of cake before we even think about picking up the fork.

Our conscious awareness of the decision is followed by reasons. *I chose this because...*

After that it's a story we're telling ourselves.

Action doesn't try to justify itself. Taking action means you're not explaining action. It means that you are adjusting course based on what is happening—not based on stories about what is happening.

PART III: NON-ACTION AS ACTION

"Act without action."

◼ TAO TE CHING ◼

ACTION AS BEARING PAIN

In Steven Pressfield's telling of the battle of Thermopylae—made famous by excitable high school teachers and Zach Snyder's *300*—Leonidas, the Spartan king, did not select the 300 soldiers based on their courage. Instead, he selected them based on the courage of their women. The ones who would be staying home.

If the mothers and wives collapsed in grief when their sons and husbands didn't come home then all of Sparta would fall. Their weakness would spread and sink the city-state.

Leonidas knew the importance of the inner battle as well as the external one.

3 THINGS THAT AREN'T ACTIONS

Perhaps we can get a better understanding of what right actions are if we look at what they are not.

■ *Ruminating.* The thought spirals that are useless. They are pure perception without any progress.

■ *Useless repetition.* A bad habit, an ineffective action, constant empty promises. Some things benefit from repetition (exercise, healthy eating, playing piano) and some do not (every mistake we make). It takes action to change course once we've created a rut for ourselves—inaction allows us to keep rolling through it.

■ *Retreat.* When we flinch and don't push back we've refused to take action. This is the automatic response to approaching a girl at a bar, selling your services for the first time, or offering up a controversial answer at a meeting. There is something deep in us that pulls back, that tells us to stay seated and shut up. Action overcomes it.

ACTION IS WAITING

The most difficult action to take is often non-action. Not stillness out of laziness, but out of self-discipline.

Waiting to look at your phone until your date is over. Waiting for the other guy to stumble in a negotiation. Waiting to work out until your injury is healed.

The sniper must be patient. Warren Buffett says he makes mistakes every time he is bored with too much money.

The Spartans would wait for their opponents to charge. They would stand still while the opposing army charged yelling and screaming. Then they would slowly, methodically, move into the charging force. The Spartans' energy was focused and tore into their scattered opponents.

Patience is an action. Laziness is not.

MEDITATION AS ACTION

Meditation connects the mind to reality.

It is pure action. There is no frustration of what should be done. There is only doing.

Meditation is a right action that acts as a catalyst for more right action.

How do you meditate?

One way: Sit down. Set a timer for twenty minutes. Close your eyes. Feel the sensation of air flowing in and out of your nostrils and on your upper lip. Each time your mind wanders bring it back to the sensation. Do not get upset when your mind wanders; the point is to become more aware of your thoughts, not get rid of them. And whatever you do, don't get upset at being upset.

CONSUMPTION AS ACTION

There is a certain amount of research you must do on something in order to effectively take action. How much? Always less than you think.

How do you know if you are reading as an action or as a way to avoid action? Are you ready to change your behavior if what you read provides a compelling enough argument to do so?

Are you engaged in the reading like you would be in a conversation with your most interesting friend?

If you can feel changes taking place within you, then you are reading as an action. If you feel like you're having a conversation with the author, then you are reading as an action. When you are immersed, you are reading as action.

Ironically, many people are more active while reading a fictional story they enjoy than a "practical" book that is boring to them.

IN YOUR BONES

I went on a ten-day meditation retreat. There was no reading, writing, or talking. Only eating sparsely, walking, and meditating.

Before going I had read plenty about meditation. I studied Eastern religions. I hung out with yogis. I even meditated twenty minutes a day.

But it wasn't until I went to the retreat that I really *understood* what it was all about.

Before the retreat I understood these ideas intellectually. Afterwards, I knew them in my bones.

All the lessons that were clichés became authentic.

Through practice (*praxis!*), theory becomes reality. While the theory provided a framework for understanding, the experiences could have stood alone. The theory, not so much.

RELAXATION AS ACTION

Relaxation, when done properly, is right action.

It is the recharge you need after vigorous action.

When you become antsy you've been relaxing too long. If you were antsy going in, you shouldn't be relaxing.

Your muscles need to repair after you work out. If you work them too hard too often they will stop getting stronger. They will get smaller and weaker. The recovery is as important as the workout.

Your mind does not stop learning when you rest. In fact, your subconscious will never get to work if you don't shut your conscious mind up for a minute. Creative answers often come when we are at rest.

Relaxation doesn't mean vacation. It may be casual reading or a slow, long walk.

Einstein was famous for solving problems while playing his violin.

Of course, most violinists don't solve physics problems. The difference is that Einstein would work on a problem intensely before playing. Then he would give his mind over to playing (which was easy for him, he began playing as a boy) while his subconscious went to work sorting out what his conscious had been working on.

Relaxation can only be useful and pleasurable when it's needed. Vigorous action followed by regular respite.

IMAGINATION IS ACTION

Albert Einstein was a theoretical physicist. He used imagination to come up with theories (and then would usually make a suggestion of an experiment for other scientists to do). Einstein's imagination was not meant as an escape from reality (although it was an escape from personal drama) but to deepen his connection to reality. If his ideas were disproved, as many were, he moved on.

Nikola Tesla had a similar methodology:

> *"My method is different. I do not rush into actual work. When I get a new idea, I start at once building it up in my imagination, and make improvements and operate the device in my mind. When I have gone so far as to embody everything in my invention, every possible improvement I can think of, and when I see no fault anywhere, I put into concrete form the final product of my brain."*

Do not confuse this kind of mental work as daydreaming. The imagination is working with a goal of bringing its creations into the physical world. Einstein and Tesla were working to create structures *in* their minds so that they could export them *from* their minds.

Are you visualizing something that you will attempt to construct, or are you living in the abstract because you're afraid?

VISUALIZATION IS ACTION

> *"I don't think I could possibly do a jump, or especially a new trick, without having this imagery process. For me, this is so very key to the athlete I have become."*
>
> ◼ **EMILY COOK, OLYMPIC AERIALIST SKIER** ◼

This is action in the mind.

Visualization empowers Olympians like Emily to execute under the high-stress environment in which she competes.

You can never *fully* visualize the future. Of course the event never goes exactly as athletes plan. There are too many factors to take into account. Randomness doesn't retreat—it continues to throw obstacles in their way.

But visualization creates a space for athletes to more effectively respond.

It can do the same for us.

Visualization creates neural connections that can change the way we see situations and, subsequently, how we answer back.

It is invisible action pushing visible action.

Tonight, try seeing yourself waking up doing your first productive task—be it working out, meditating, etc.—and see if it's easier to get going than most mornings.

OBSERVATION IS ACTION

We can benefit from the actions of others as well as our own.

When you look around you can see all sorts of things. If you want to learn about getting girls, go to the bar and observe interactions. If you want to learn about giving a great speech, watch presidential speeches or watch a TED talk for its delivery instead of its content.

If you want to start a business it's more useful to mimic an entrepreneur you admire than reading a book on the subject (both are useful). If you want to get fit, watch to see what the most ripped person in the gym is doing and try that.

It's best to go to the source. Don't ask the Olympian how they're so good. They probably don't know (but they definitely think they do). Instead, watch them. How do they hold themselves? What is their practice regimen? What is their diet? What are their beliefs?

BITTERSWEET EPIPHANIES

The sad part of an epiphany is realizing that you were not the first person to have it. Not even close. (This is referring to wide-reaching epiphanies rather than epiphanies about an individual situation.)

Philosophers have been saying that for thousands of years. There are fifty other startups doing nearly the same thing. There are already three hundred books written on the topic.

Your chance to be unique is in the actions you take *after* the epiphany. Nobody will be able to execute like you.

The power of an epiphany is determined by the power of the actions that follow.

PART IV: DOING ACTION

"The fire-fly only shines when on the wing; so it is with the mind; when we rest we darken."

■ PHILIP JAMES BAILEY ■

SOME ACTIONS HAVE MORE LEVERAGE

◼ *Habits.* Most of our life is shaped by our habits. Our eating habits, thinking habits, working habits, and every other default we have. When you focus on shaping your default actions you multiply the effect of the action. For instance, the first day you eat well will be hard but will feel good. The twentieth day you eat well it will be easier. The fiftieth day you won't even be thinking about it.

◼ *Environment.* Some actions create a more healthy environment. Making a new group of friends may change things forever. Putting up a poster reminding you to take action today will change your life far into the future. Cleaning your desk will make you more sane for a week (or until it gets destroyed again). These are actions that you will benefit from daily.

◼ *Experiments.* If you consciously measure the outcome of an action then it will matter more. You can learn better from actions that are meant to test a hypothesis. Remember, "What gets measured gets managed."

THE HARP

When you learn to play a song on a harp you know that you will pluck some strings and not others. There is a correct order to play the strings in order to get the sound you want.

You have to play some wrong strings before you play just right ones.

You don't fear the wrong strings, you just know that they aren't useful for achieving your goal.

Don't fear the wrong actions, just work patiently towards finding the right ones.

Don't fear the negative thought, just work patiently towards the more productive one.

THE HALF-WAY GLASS

There's been a lot of concern with a certain glass over the years. It's 50% filled with water.

Some people think it is half full, others see half empty.

There's a room full of people arguing about the fullness or emptiness of the thing. A kid walks in, drinks what's there, and then fills it up. The room goes quiet.

That's the only person taking action.

INTELLIGENT IGNORANCE

Every teenager believes he knows everything and every veteran scientist knows he knows next-to-nothing.

We stagnate when we think we need to know everything (the exception being that overconfident teen). When we feel we need complete information we won't make a move.

When we take action we accept that it might not work.

We accept our ignorance without fearing it.

ASYMMETRIC OUTCOMES

If I practiced piano I could go a long time with no progress (longer than normal, my musical talent is horrifyingly close to zero) and then one day something would click and there would seem to be an instant increase in skill.

There are few activities with a perfect relationship between progress and perspiration over the long term. Plateaus are a fact of life.

Anybody who has remained committed to an activity for a long period of time knows that you go through plateaus. It doesn't look like you're making any progress, and by any measurement you aren't, but then one day something clicks and you break through to a whole new level of performance.

These plateaus are the most difficult to continue through. It doesn't seem as if our effort is getting us anywhere.

We get worried that the plateau doesn't end—that it's actually just a long, low peak.

It's important that we focus on the action, the *process*.

Maybe there is something holding you back. Maybe you need another point of view. Maybe, in fact, quitting *is* the best action to take.

Ask others in the field, "Did you also experience a plateau like this?"

HEROIC ACTION

> *"What matters to an active man is to do the right thing; whether the right thing comes to pass should not bother him."*
>
> ■ **GOETHE** ■

Ancient heroes were judged by their actions instead of the results.

Imagine your favorite fictional character acting just as they do, but failing. Would that take anything away from the person? Of course not.

Much of life is random—including extreme success.

Sometimes the dragon burns down our house while we're sleeping. Sometimes we get caught in a crossfire. In fact, there are few obstacles we can know for sure.

Do not let this randomness (unfairness) of results wear you down or induce you to cut ethical corners.

Focus on acting in the way you know you should, regardless of the circumstances.

Focus on the actions you take, not on their outcome or payoff.

The payoff may give you information on what to do next, but not on who you should be next.

"SUCCESSFUL PEOPLE _____"

There are thousands of bloggers filling in that blank space every day.

Millions click the headline hoping for *the* answer. The one that was missing the last hundred times they clicked a nearly identical headline.

Successful people are humans. Meaning they do all the wrong things: they ignore the emotional needs of their spouses, they abandon their children, they go insane, they procrastinate, they eat poorly and drink too much, they have negative thoughts, they waste money, they're shortsighted, they're everything you are and worse.

Read a couple biographies. Walt Disney chain-smoked, is rumored to have sympathized with Nazis, and was a terrible boss. Steve Jobs would tell an employee his idea was terrible and then present it as his own the next day. Warren Buffett drinks five Cherry Cokes a day, lived with another woman while married, and refused to acknowledge his son's adopted kids as family members. Quentin Tarantino nearly drove his friend to suicide because he was such a competitive movie buff.

Everybody screws up. Everybody, for that matter, *is* screwed up.

Nobody is winning because they're perfect. They're winning because they have consistently taken action, they have remained focused, and, more often than you'd think, they got lucky.

Stop worrying about having all your ducks in a row, "getting your life together," or whatever else it is.

Today move in the direction you want to move in. Take action.

The world around you is a mess, have fun with it.

RITUAL

When something has survived for thousands of years, there is a reason. There is a deeper rationality to what seems irrational.

Rituals—religious, philosophical, creative, and otherwise—can often provide peace, strength, and inspiration much more potently than talking, reading, or statically thinking.

Why?

Rituals are based in action.

They create a movement or symbolism that we can attach our ideas to.

Rituals are essentially habitual movements that bring us to a certain headspace. Consistent actions affecting the mind.

Many great creative minds have relied on rituals. Stephen King discusses his:

> *"There are certain things I do if I sit down to write. I have a glass of water or a cup of tea. There's a certain time I sit down, from eight to eight thirty, somewhere within that half hour every morning. I have my vitamin pill and my music, sit in the same seat, and the papers are all arranged in the same places."*

Rituals are poetic habits. They serve a purpose that may not make sense to the reasoning mind—but is undeniable to the heart.

REACTIVITY

Right action is not reactive, it is proactive. It is independent of others' immediate demands on your time.

Checking email, Facebook, and Twitter upon waking up sets you up for a day of reactivity. Starting the day with your own creative labor sets you up for a day of action.

What's the most important thing you could work on today? Why aren't you putting that before everything else?

It's hard. But only until you begin.

STEPPING FORWARD

You must be willing to change everything on the evidence of new information (or even a gut instinct). As Emerson wrote in *Self-Reliance,* "A foolish consistency is the hobgoblin of little minds..."

The legendary investor George Soros is known for holding a strong opinion on a certain market and then taking a position in the opposite direction the next day. He's not afraid to change his mind when new information is available.

Each action you take provides a new view. You may discover something about the world (or yourself) that completely changes the course of action you must take. You change and the world changes. Don't fear contradicting yourself.

How do we avoid the fear of being misunderstood—that feeling that we are a traitor to some idea or plan? We act into it.

As soon as you dive into the new path of action you answer all of the worries you had. Is this really the correct path? Well, it's your new best guess—try and find out.

Do not get stuck at crossroads. Remember that you have all the information that you will have from where you stand, then pick.

There may be no right answer but by now you know the one definitely wrong answer: standing still.

SATISFICE

Nobel Prize winner Herbert Simon postulated that people can be divided into two groups: Maximizers and Satisficers.

Whether they're choosing a restaurant, college, or spouse, maximizers are obsessed with always making the very best choice and trying to attain the very fullest happiness.

Satisficers are happy with any sufficient option.

You'd think Maximizers would be happier, since they spend so much time and energy on making the best possible choice.

But they're not.

Even after they make their choice, they agonize that maybe it wasn't the right one after all.

Satisficers, meanwhile, have moved on with their life and are enjoying what they chose.

Deciding is progress.

Perfect is the enemy of good.

WARREN BUFFETT DIDN'T HAVE A PLAN

Warren Buffett was obsessed with making money his whole life. It became his favorite game. Many focus on making money to buy things; these people often lead extremely unhappy lives. They can never *have* enough.

Warren Buffett is insatiable as well, but his focus is on the game. Therefore he could never *play* enough. It wasn't about acquisition; it was about playing the game.

Popular self-help would have us believe that without a master plan our lives will surely be worth nothing.

Yet Buffett admits at the end of *The Snowball*, his fantastic biography, that he had no plan early on.

His laser focus and love for money-making ensured a future where Buffett would amass a fortune. The path he would take to do that, however, was just as uncertain as yours.

PROBABILITIES

> *"You are not a lottery ticket."*
>
> ◼ PETER THIEL ◼

Our ability to determine probabilities is weaker than we can imagine.

When you look at the possibility of your success in an endeavor, it's dangerous to look at the success rate of everyone who ever attempted it before.

The failure rate in any given field is *in general*. You may have a knack that sets you apart, you may have resources that others haven't been able to draw on, you may be putting in more effort than 90% of the others.

A statistic can give you a measurement of the failure and success rate of a certain thing, but it hides an amazing amount of details about what went into each attempt.

What you're capable of can't be calculated.

EXPLANATIONS

> *"We cannot spend the day in explanation."*
>
> ◼ **RALPH WALDO EMERSON** ◼
> *SELF-RELIANCE*

We try to explain everything. Why we are where we are. Why our parents raised us that way. What everything means. Why that happened to us and why nothing is fair.

We allow our minds to run in circles of bitching and moaning and then wonder why we feel too tired to make anything happen. We leave ourselves zero energy left to deal with the *actual* problems (which probably are way different than the ones we imagined).

Instead of asking "Why?" leave it at "Why not?"

LUXURIOUS INACTION

Some are born without the luxury to be lazy. They had to take action or die.

The enviable position isn't always as enviable as we think. Nature does a great job at balancing out everything.

Those who "never had to work a day in their life" end up being soft in body, mind, and spirit.

Most of the millionaires I know personally came from nothing.

They were forced to focus on money from an early age. They never questioned their dedication to making money because it was so precious growing up.

Inaction is a luxury, one that many take for granted (and take pills to deal with). Action comes from hardship and necessity, physical or psychological.

If you were born into luxury, or earned it later, the trick is to treat it with disdain and effort with reverence.

To stay hungry when you could be constantly full—to stay active when you could be sedate.

KEEP MOVING

Amelia Earhart had the phrase "Always think with your stick forward" painted on the side of her plane. If she slowed down too much she would crash.

Einstein wrote in a letter to his son, who was in a downward mental spiral, that "life is like riding a bicycle" because you can't stop.

There are some species of shark that have to continually swim forward to breathe.

Humans are the same way—we have to keep moving or we die.

PERSISTENCE AND INEVITABILITY

Persistent action is proof to the world and ourselves that we will not be stopped—by failure, setbacks, external circumstances, doubts, anything. It may be ugly. It may not be quick. It *is* inevitable.

Time works for anyone who is willing to persist.

That Rocky quote is true: "[I]t ain't about how hard you hit. It's about how hard you can get hit and keep moving forward; how much you can take and keep moving forward. That's how winning is done!"

One of Warren Buffett's few rules is having a large margin of error. He knows that retaining capital is more important than massive gains because without the capital there's nothing to invest.

You build power and momentum as you act, you lose it as you stagnate. This accumulates through your consistency. If you get up every time you're knocked down you're guaranteed to at least die on your feet.

"JUST TAKE IT BIRD BY BIRD."

"Thirty years ago my older brother, who was ten years old at the time, was trying to get a report on birds written that he'd had three months to write [which] was due the next day. We were out at our family cabin in Bolinas, and he was at the kitchen table close to tears, surrounded by binder paper and pencils and unopened books on birds, immobilized by the hugeness of the task ahead. Then my father sat down beside him, put his arm around my brother's shoulder, and said, 'Bird by bird, buddy. Just take it bird by bird.'"

■ ANNE LAMOTT, *BIRD BY BIRD* ■

When you think of all that needs to be done to get from where you are to where you want to be—to reach a big goal or complete an audacious project—it can be overwhelming. So much so that you feel paralyzed and unable to start at all.

Just take things "bird by bird." Action by action.

Don't look ahead. Concentrate solely on the very first step.

Once it's done, take the next step. And the next. And the next.

Until you arrive.

IT MAY NOT HAPPEN

Einstein became famous for his Theory of Relativity in his thirties. After that he would spend most of his energies on trying (and failing) to debunk quantum physics and trying (and failing) to solve his Unified Field Theory.

He set himself a second set of pyramids to construct and, in the end, couldn't.

Maybe that's because it was impossible.

There is a possibility that the thing we're aiming at may not be attainable—it may not even be a possibility.

Would that rob all of our actions of their meaning? Absolutely not.

Many of the greatest discoveries occurred on accident. Penicillin and silly putty, to name just two.

PART V:
BENEFITS OF ACTION

"Action may not always bring happiness; but there is no happiness without action."

■ **BENJAMIN DISRAELI** ■

ACTION SHUTS UP FALSE MORALS

We often think we don't take action because we fear failure.

I don't think we do. We've been failing since we were born. We failed to walk. We failed to make the team. We failed to properly write an "A." We were born into a life of constant failing. Every day is a failure to be who you will be tomorrow.

Sure, at some point we start feeling ashamed of failure. I'm not convinced that's what we're actually afraid of, though. So what are we actually afraid of?

Being rejected. By the tribe. By the boss. By the girl. By the audience. By the mob. These things set our amygdalas on fire.

Humans need humans.

We fear that if we do what we want we will step on other people's toes. We might take a wrong turn and be rejected. If you are fully yourself, the tribe may label you an outcast and you'll never be included again.

If we fail, we're guaranteed to get love. Failures who followed the rules are forgiven. The ones who go out and disrupt the natural order, no way.

Action shuts up the mind that is concerned with rules. Action is concerned with creation. It's concerned with what *is,* not what *should be.*

ACTION KILLS ADDICTION

We're addicted to everything. There are literally chemicals that compel us to stay on reddit looking at cat pictures. Every novelty squirts little chemicals into our system. We have to fight it (if we can't avoid it).

We're addicted to compliments and looking at other people living their lives on Facebook. We're addicted to TV shows and sugar. We're addicted to running away from the thing we know we should be doing.

It takes one moment of strength to ignore the addiction and take action.

You stop craving ice cream five minutes into a run.

The itch to check Instagram ebbs the minute you turn off your phone.

As soon as you start, the addiction is destroyed.

ACTION BREATHES LIFE INTO CLICHÉS

We know clichés are there for a reason. Maybe they aren't all correct, but they've served some purpose for a long time.

We can't truly appreciate them, though, until we have direct experience. Until we come face to face with something that makes us say, *"That's* what grandpa was talking about all those years."

ACTION PUTS TIME ON YOUR SIDE

"[H]e not busy being born is busy dying."

■ BOB DYLAN ■

Time works against anything that is stagnant. Machines that aren't used rust. Water that stays still turns to poison. Sharks that don't swim suffocate.

When you take action you are putting time on your side. You are ensuring that you learn with time. That time gives you more opportunities instead of diminishing them. Action uses time to create new potentialities and even new lives.

ACTION IS GENIUS

Einstein said, "It's not that I'm so smart, it's just that I stay with problems longer." He first envisioned himself riding along with a light beam when he was a young boy. That vision stuck with him into his thirties. He couldn't stop thinking about it until he could explain it.

Thomas Edison has given us many clichés about the importance of hard work—the truth of which, like all clichés, you don't really understand until you've lived them through action. A favorite:

> *"Genius is one percent inspiration, ninety-nine percent perspiration."*

Friedrich Nietzsche had a poetic way of saying the same thing:

> *"Do not talk about giftedness, inborn talents! One can name great men of all kinds who were very little gifted! They acquired greatness, became 'geniuses' (as we put it), through qualities the lack of which no one who knew what they were would boast of: they all possessed that seriousness of the efficient workman which first learns to construct the parts properly before it ventures to fashion a great whole; they allowed themselves time for it, because they took more pleasure in making the little, secondary things well than in the effect of a dazzling whole."*

Scott Fitzgerald points to the "dazzling whole" referred to by Nietzsche here:

> *"Genius is the ability to put into effect what is in your mind."*

Action is required to slowly build the bridge from imagination to reality. Your craft is your chosen tool to express what is in your mind. It will be frustratingly bad at first. It is only with diligent practice that we can sharpen the tool and see more defined expressions of our mind in the external world.

ACTION IS INSPIRATION

Many of the greatest writers explain their creative process as sitting down and writing. It's the effort that opens you up for inspiration.

Nobody achieves greatness except through intense practice over a long period of time.

We try to get around this. We see people whose first novel was a bestseller or who created a successful first business venture. We should be them. What our stories rarely include is the time that these prodigies put in ahead of time. Left out is the sacrifice and pain they've suffered personally because of their intense dedication.

Inspiration comes to those who work.

"*There is a muse, but he's not going to come fluttering down into your writing room and scatter creative fairy-dust all over your typewriter or computer. He lives in the ground. He's a basement kind of guy. You have to descend to his level, and once you get down there you have to furnish an apartment for him to live in. You have to do all the grunt labor, in other words, while the muse sits and smokes cigars and admires his bowling trophies and pretends to ignore you. Do you think it's fair? I think it's fair. He may not be much to look at, that muse-guy, and he may not be much of a conversationalist, but he's got inspiration. It's right that you should do all the work and burn all the mid-night oil, because the guy with the cigar and the little wings has got a bag of magic. There's stuff in there that can change your life. Believe me, I know.*"

■ **STEPHEN KING,** *ON WRITING* ■

ACTION IS INSPIRATION: PART II

You don't need another motivational quote laid over a picture of a mountain. Think about what happens every time you go on a motivational image or video binge. You jump from image to image, releasing a little more dopamine with each click (like an addict).

Then you get to a point maybe an hour later and realize that all the motivation did was kill time. Now you're exhausted and have no energy to do anything else.

A much better way to inspire yourself is to take action.

Work on your project. Take the first step towards starting a new habit. Write the first paragraph of a blog post.

Do something!

The only information that stays inspiring in the long-run is the information that we apply.

Knowledge is not power, it's frustration. *Applied* knowledge is power.

When your default is action, inspiration builds on itself.

SNOWBALL

> *"It's not the load that breaks you down, it's the way you carry it."*
>
> ◼ **LENA HORNE** ◼

Warren Buffett became one of the richest men in the world by following each of his actions to the next. He didn't do it all at once.

He started where he was and then moved slowly and methodically. His biggest advantage: not making greedy (stupid) mistakes.

No large project is completed in one movement. There are multiple moving pieces that must follow a particular order.

It's unrealistic to think that you will adopt all the good habits you think you should today. You may have one great day and then are sure to fall off the horse. In order to build strong habits you must start with a single habit. Practice it diligently until you do it without thinking. Only then do you move on to the next habit.

Small consistent action beats single Herculean leaps (almost) every time.

ACTION IS PASSION

> *"The more we focused on loving what we do, the less we ended up loving it."*
>
> ■ CAL NEWPORT ■
> *SO GOOD THEY CAN'T IGNORE YOU*

Most people should not quit their jobs and go "do what they love" for the simple reason that most people can't make money doing what they love.

And they'll stop loving what they love when they try to make money from it.

Maybe they'd start loving what they *do* do if they stopped feeling like they should be doing something else.

Instead of finding your passion, and then getting to work, get to work, and you might find your passion.

ACTION FINDS FALSE DREAMS

One way we protect ourselves from failure is by guaranteeing it.

We embrace a dream that is so audacious we will certainly fail. This gives us a certain amount of solace.

I never stood a chance anyways.

This answer doesn't satisfy anyone dedicated to right action, though. There was no learning, no hypothesis to test, no uncertainty, no risk.

We felt safe in predicting a failure that we could ensure.

Right action guarantees progress. Even in the face of a sabotaging unconscious.

ACTION MAKES YOU BIG

Action means you've risked being wrong. You've put your skin in the game.

By having something to lose, you separate yourself from those on the sidelines.

> "A lesson I learned from this ancient [Greek] culture is the notion of megalopsychon (a term expressed in Aristotle's ethics), a sense of grandeur that was superseded by the Christian value of 'humility.' There is no word for it in Romance languages; in Arabic is called Shhm—best translated as non-small. If you take risks and face your fate with dignity, there is nothing you can do that makes you small; if you don't take risks, there is nothing you can do that makes you grand, nothing. And when you take risks, insults by half-men (small men, those who don't risk anything) are similar to barks by nonhuman animals: you can't feel insulted by a dog."
>
> ■ **NASSIM TALEB,** *THE BLACK SWAN* ■

HOW TO CREATE COURAGE

> *"Courage is not something that you already have that makes you brave when the tough times start. Courage is what you earn when you've been through the tough times and you discover they aren't so tough after all."*
>
> ■ MALCOLM GLADWELL ■
> *DAVID AND GOLIATH*

Forget about sacking up or being a chicken or a bitch or pussy or coward.

Forget about getting the courage.

Forget about your mindset for a minute.

Act. Distract yourself from how scary the thing is by being so deeply involved in it there's not room for anything else.

Then later, after you've been beaten down, failed, and cried, you'll look up and see what you've done. The messy progress you've made. The unplannable zig-zagging course you took to get here. The brave heart you've earned.

You'll have forgotten why you were ever afraid.

ACTION CALLS DOWN THE ASSISTANCE OF THE GODS

"Until one is committed, there is hesitancy, the chance to draw back, always ineffectiveness. Concerning all acts of initiative (and creation), there is one elementary truth the ignorance of which kills countless ideas and splendid plans: that the moment one definitely commits oneself, then providence moves too. A whole stream of events issues from the decision, raising in one's favor all manner of unforeseen incidents, meetings and material assistance, which no man could have dreamt would have come his way. I learned a deep respect for one of Goethe's couplets:

'Whatever you can do or dream you can, begin it. Boldness has genius, power and magic in it!'"

■ **W. H. MURRAY** ■

There is a magic in action. Christians call it God. Emerson called it the Oversoul. There are a thousand other names. Nobody can pretend it's not there.

Every time I've begun taking actions toward a goal, my environment and other people have helped me in unanticipated ways. Maybe people are just drawn to somebody who knows what they want. Maybe when you know what you want you are able to more easily see and get the things you need. I don't know.

It feels like magic.

"I learned this, at least, by my experiment: that if one advances confidently in the direction of his dreams, and endeavors to live the life which he has imagined, he will meet with a success unexpected in common hours...If you have built castles in the air, your work need not be lost; that is where they should be. Now put the foundations under them."

■ **HENRY DAVID THOREAU,** *WALDEN* ■

EMERGENCE

Action creates new possibilities that didn't exist before. Every step you take in a certain direction multiplies the opportunities for you in that direction. The opportunities in the other paths shrink away to make room.

You choose the direction in which your possible futures emerge. You don't know exactly what this will look like, but you have an idea.

Emergence is a powerful force that you engage with every day. It works for both good and ill.

It's why it's so easy to stay stuck in depression. Every step into depression creates new, darker possibilities.

On the other hand, every step towards a healthy mind and body creates new potential in health. Every healthy meal, workout, or positive thought creates an opening for more.

Those who can see one business opportunity can see a thousand. Those who write daily never run out of ideas. Those who hate themselves hate the world.

You get to choose. Every day. Every hour.

ACTION BALANCES PAST, PRESENT, AND FUTURE

When we are thinking, it is almost always about the past or the future. The present gets lost. Thoughts don't have much to do in the present moment. Everything seems to be safe in the present moment, there's nothing to worry about. There's nothing to regret in the present, either. So they go off time-traveling and find things to worry and dream about.

There is a time for this, of course. We need to reflect. We need to plan. Unfortunately, we default to expending all our energy on these things. Focusing ourselves on action puts the past, present, and future back into balance.

ACTION FOCUSES YOUR MIND ON CREATION

When you act (putting some knowledge into action, practicing, making, tinkering, whatever) you force your mind into the creative mode. It is now becoming better at something. It is now making something.

You have, in an instant, switched from a consumption mindset to a creation mindset. From a fixed mindset to a growth mindset.

ACTION TRIGGERS YOUR INTUITION

Steve Jobs said, "I began to realize that an intuitive understanding and consciousness was more significant than abstract thinking and intellectual logical analysis." Indeed!

How do we develop our intuitive sense? Action!

There are exercises like meditation and stream-of-consciousness writing that are worth practicing to hone our intuitions as well; yet there is no better way to develop our intuition than taking action.

If you want to develop an intuition for making decisions quickly, then practice making decisions! Force yourself to a 30-second time limit for any non-life-threatening decision.

The sign of a true master is the ability to do the work without seeming to have to think about it. The reason the master doesn't have to think is because he has internalized all the processes of the task. His intuition drives his actions.

(Note that intuitions are specific to one's area of mastery. The chef has intuition about how things will taste, the general has intuitions about when to attack, and the psychologist has intuitions about what may help a person's psyche.)

Action develops your sixth sense.

ACTION PUTS YOU INTO THE FLOW STATE

Once the details of whatever your craft is are internalized you are capable of entering the flow state. This is the mental state that allows for the greatest human achievement. Athletes and traders call it being "in the zone."

It also happens to be the state in which we find the most happiness.

We don't *feel* happy in the moment of flow, but we later describe it as a "peak" experience.

This state is readily available for anyone who has put in many hours of focused, deliberate practice. That is, focused action.

ACTION PRIORITIZES CONSUMPTION

We are in an age worse than yellow journalism. Everyone is desperate for your attention. If you're not purposeful, you will spend your entire life consuming meaningless content.

The internet has put the focus of journalism on a clickable headline with shareable content. Being useful or informative is no longer a priority of the media.

My Facebook wall has been making some pretty audacious promises: "The One Thing You Need To Know To Be Successful," "The Four Steps To Transform Your Business," "This Superfruit Will Melt Away Fat!"

People email us demanding our time. Our friends expect us to watch fifty different TV shows. I still have to take that one course to learn that other thing.

There is an amazing amount of information out there. At best, we can consume about zero percent of it.

When we focus on taking action it becomes obvious what we should read and what shows matter to us (if any).

When I began writing this book I immediately stopped reading four books I was in the middle of. I also severely limited my time on email and Facebook, and deleted all the apps on my phone meant for consumption (except for the Kindle app—reading Marcus Aurelius' *Meditations* was part of the research for this book).

Focusing on action acts as a powerful filter for your information and entertainment consumption—limiting the time you spend on it and directing your attention to that with the most value.

FORTUNE-TELLING

"Narrow-minded prediction has an analgesic or therapeutic effect. Be aware of the numbing effect of magic numbers. Be prepared for all relevant eventualities."

◼ **NASSIM TALEB,** *THE BLACK SWAN* ◼

It feels good to pretend we know what will happen. We want to believe that we can predict the future.

We will ignore every piece of evidence of the future and hang on to words of false prophets.

Action helps us avoid this false sense of confidence. It hardens us to what may come.

It allows us to prepare for the future while admitting that we don't know what will happen.

ACTION ALLOWS SERENDIPITY

Horace Walpole coined the term *serendipity* after reading the Persian fairytale *The Three Princes of Serendip*. The princes in the story "were always making discoveries, by accidents and sagacity, of things they were not in quest of."

If the princes sat at home bored they would never make any exciting discoveries. If they were so focused on their quest that it blinded their mind to what was around them, then they would miss many opportunities.

Instead, they kept their eyes open for hidden opportunities as they moved along.

Serendipity is not available to the stagnant or the narrow-minded—only the open and aware.

ACTION CREATES BEAUTY

Action doesn't allow for the prettiness of a porcelain doll. Action is not for those who wish to appear untouched and unused.

Action is beautiful because of the mess it leaves. The zig-zagging path. The scarred face. The broken heart. The true confidence that can only come with experience.

Action creates the kind of beauty that deepens with time, not the façade of beauty that fights time with botox.

HUMILITY

"My wish for you, Kallistos, is that you survive as many battles in the flesh as you have already fought in your imagination. Perhaps then you will acquire the humility of a man and bear yourself no longer as the demigod you presume yourself to be."

■ **DIENEKES** ■
IN STEVEN PRESSFIELD'S *GATES OF FIRE*

Your imagination can go forward without the body, but your body cannot leave your mind behind. The battles of the flesh are also of the mind.

Reading a book may send your imagination years ahead to an ideal future where you've made no mistakes. Where you deal with hardship flawlessly without effort.

Knowledge without practice can create a kind of arrogance that is dangerous. The same is true for the successful beginner. If your first venture is wildly successful you will believe you can do no wrong. This will make you reckless in your second venture. You will be blind to weaknesses in your own plan and to the strengths of your competitors.

Action teaches us that nobody is invincible. Those who think they are, live in abstraction and leave themselves vulnerable.

LEAN ACTIONS

The business world at large is refocusing on action over abstraction. Eric Ries documents this transformation and lays out the general framework for its management methodology in his great book *The Lean Startup.*

One of the fundamental keys he discusses is the "minimum viable product" (MVP). This is a product that is quick and cheap to build and tests a fundamental hypothesis.

This allows a startup to prove its concept and raise money. Or fail fast and try something new without spending too much cash.

It allows established companies to continue innovating without risking their whole business.

Smart entrepreneurs and businessmen know how expensive abstraction and over-planning is; they prefer to find out the cheapest way possible—taking action.

Testing a product will show us whether or not there is a market for it.

Testing our own dream will quickly show us whether or not we really like it or what else we will need to do to accomplish it.

> *"MVPs require the courage to put one's assumptions to the test. If customers react the way we expect, we can take that as confirmation that our assumptions are correct."*
>
> ◼ ERIC RIES ◼

Of course, most tests don't go our way. That's why we have to make them cheap. That's why we have to pay attention.

TESTING THE DOUBTERS

With the lowered costs of trying things, it means the value of listening to doubters is at a historic low.

They don't know what's possible.

You don't either.

Your effort and audacity to run the test will let you know for sure.

It's not about knowing what will work. It's about finding out.

FOCUS ON SOLUTIONS

"So what does it matter when the cause of the darkness differs?"

■ PERICLES ■

Action directs your attention to figuring out solutions instead of playing with causes (with no roots).

The story behind something often matters less than we think. Better to deal with the thing as it is.

LEAN ACTIONS: PART II

> *"As you consider building your own minimum viable product, let this simple rule suffice: remove any feature, process, or effort that does not contribute directly to the learning you seek."*
>
> ■ ERIC RIES ■

Startups focus their tests to answer their most important questions. You should, too.

There tends to be an inverse relationship between what is important in our life and how much attention we give it. It's kind of sick.

Focus on answering the questions that are driving you most crazy.

What do I want to do for a living?

Go and try different jobs at the lowest level. What do you enjoy doing? What environments do feel at home in? What profession has the people in it you like best?

Why am I so out of shape?

Stop eating *that*. Start working out. Stop reading about fitness until you've made a habit out of the first two.

Why can't I get a significant other?

Try going on dates. Pay attention. You'll find out.

Treat your life as an experiment. Train yourself to run tests as quickly and cheaply as possible.

Tests don't last forever. Give it two weeks. You can do anything for two weeks.

"All life is an experiment. The more experiments you make the better."

■ **RALPH WALDO EMERSON** ■

ERROR BECOMES INFORMATION

When right action doesn't work, it provides you information.

Scientists know this well. Mostly because their failure rates are extraordinarily high.

A good scientist sees more in his failures than his successes. His successes come out of failures.

The rest of us aren't different, we just think we are.

ACTION SHOWS US WHAT WE'RE CAPABLE OF (AND WHAT WE'RE NOT...YET)

Our neocortex is good at a lot of things. Its prophesying capabilities have launched us well beyond any other species we know of when it comes to thinking.

One thing it's *not* so good at is determining our abilities. Our ego will either blow our capabilities out of proportion or shrink them into something shameful. For most of us, it errs on the shameful side.

Instead of guessing, try. See where your weaknesses lie. Identify your strengths.

ACTION SHOWS YOU WHAT YOUR PLAN IS WORTH

The Wright Brothers were trying to make a flying machine. So was everybody else. The difference? The Wright Brothers had a thousand dollars to work with while the others had millions.

This doesn't make any sense. Massive corporations with hundreds of scientists and engineers should have easily destroyed these two bicycle-building brothers. They didn't though because of one more key difference: The Wright Brothers had as many test flights in a single month (1,900) than their corporate rivals had in a year. How!?

By focusing on action. They would make a failed test flight then make minor adjustments to their original plans. They would soon be ready for the next test flight and repeat the process again. And again. Their big-budget competitors would go back to the drawing board with each failed attempt, wasting massive amounts of time and money.

The Wright Brothers' focus on action allowed them to learn more quickly and get to an answer. Their competitors' focus on planning made them slow, expensive, and ultimately less effective.

Action demonstrates what works better than an abstract idea.

ACTION IS LEARNING

To repeat:

You never forget anything you learn on your own.

All secondary experiences may easily be forgotten.

ACTION MAKES SENSE OF NONSENSE

"Mental clarity is the child of courage, not the other way around."

■ **NASSIM TALEB** ■

THE BED OF PROCRUSTES

The most rational belief may feel irrational.

The world is messy, and those who think they've made sense of it are often wrong.

Right action makes sense of nonsense when abstraction would just lead to frustration.

When you act you prove whether something will work or not. You take a step. Your eyes are on the path, not on the chaos surrounding it.

Our tragic mistake: we believe that we must understand something *before* taking action when, in fact, we can only fully understand something *after* taking action.

ACTION BUILDS MOMENTUM

If you go to the gym when you're tired you will return home feeling invigorated. Tomorrow you may look forward to going (but you know you won't need to).

If you are craving the pizza but order the salad instead, you will find a sense of pride. The next healthy choice is going to be easier.

The blank page is petrifying. Halfway through the page you don't remember what "not having any ideas" feels like.

This momentum isn't invincible. Every day there are forces—within and without—to stop you. People expecting explanations, your mind telling you to take a break, you're too tired.

There is always something new to push past—consistency in action wins every time.

ACTION USES YOUR WEAKNESS

> *"To play by David's rules, you have to be desperate. You have to be so bad that you have no choice."*
>
> ◼ **MALCOLM GLADWELL** ◼
> *DAVID AND GOLIATH*

When you take action your weaknesses don't just fall away, they become useful.

Your whole life you have transformed because of your weaknesses.

The fat kid who had to get funny to be accepted in school and now has a Comedy Central Presents special.

The poor kid who had nothing got used to working hard and now runs a business with an unlimited source of energy nobody understands. (This is true of many of the strongest entrepreneurs out there. Action was never optional—they *had* to act to eat.)

The ugly girl who got made fun of got healthy and is now a Victoria's Secret Angel.

The lonely girl who had no friends and spent all her time with imaginary playmates and now writes bestselling fantasy for a living.

You know the clichés: Steve Jobs the orphan, Richard Branson the dyslexic, Jay-Z the thug, the list goes on and on.

It turns out that orphans have an advantage in life (at least in the area of achievement) because they have such strong insecurities to push against, to *compensate* for.

How have you compensated for your weaknesses? Has paying too much attention to them made them more or less trouble?

If used as launching pads for action, your greatest weaknesses can become your greatest strengths.

REGRET

Think about the things you regret. Think about the things you *know* you will regret in the future.

The most painful are the acts of *omission*. Of *not* doing something.

Those regrets last forever. They're chronic.

The pain that comes from acts of *commission* is more acute. It hurts more right away.

We regret those too.

But not for as long. And we almost always learn something. We have another dent in our armor, but we don't die.

Regret is eternal for those who don't act.

For those who do, regret ceases as soon as action begins.

ACTION IS HUMBLING

A plan, graph, or projection can make you feel invincible. *It's all there—can't you see? It's as good as done!*

Action requires you come back to reality. It forces you to see the details you overlooked. The economic forces you couldn't have predicted. The over-optimism you sold yourself on to sell your investors on.

Action is the great equalizer. It will prove to the depressed person that he is not nearly as bad as he thinks. It will prove to the manic person that they aren't nearly the god they see themselves as.

Action shows you when the emperor isn't wearing clothes.

Action forces you to deal with things not as you *want* or *believe* them to be, but as they *are*.

OPPOSITION BECOMES YOUR FUEL

> *"The impediment to action advances action. What stands in the way becomes the way."*
>
> ◼ **MARCUS AURELIUS** ◼

The hardest things you have ever done made you bigger.

Superheroes can only perform at their peak when a Supervillain comes to town.

(It's why they don't defeat them "once and for all.")

The only reason David's battle with Goliath is memorable is because it didn't *look* like David should have won.

It turns out that the underdog wins all the time—in sports, war, and business. Why? The underdog is under a greater force, so they are able to push back harder. They are able to call on energy, strength, and tactics that the comfortable could never summon.

Abstraction will show you it's impossible. Action is the process of making the impossible possible.

"You know, what I finally learned after a long time is basically if you want something enough—unless you're totally without ability—but if you want something enough, and you keep pushing toward it, you will probably get there because nobody is pushing back with the same amount of energy."

■ **ROBERT GOTTLIEB** ■
**LEGENDARY EDITOR WHO WORKED WITH
ROBERT CARO, JOSEPH HELLER, TONI MORRISON,
AND BILL CLINTON**

ACTION TEACHES WITH RESPECT

When you teach others through your actions you skip the pretense of knowing what is right for *them*. You transmit lessons by embodying them instead of trying to talk about them in a persuasive way.

There is no single correct way to live. The ways are as many as the people living.

Action teaches a general pattern rather than dictating a set path.

Action offers lessons in how, rather than what.

An education in action doesn't offer all the answers, but provides the motivation to look for them.

STOP ASKING "WHY?"

Why are you blogging? Why do you want to write a book? Why would you think people would like that? Why do you want that job? Why do you want to date that person? Why do you deserve to like your work? Why do you think anybody would care what you have to say? Why do you think your solution is worthwhile?

Why?

Stop justifying, start acting.

FRAMING

When your focus is on taking action you will notice a shift in your mind.

It is becoming primed to see opportunities in chaos.

Because it is beginning to see reality.

It's not "*What should I* think *about this?*"

It's "*What am I going to* do *about this?*"

This kind of reframing is fundamental. You can work on it in your mind, consciously reframing situations.

Or you can allow it to follow your dedication to taking action. To using whatever pieces are in front of you to build. Maybe not what you had in mind, but something.

ACTION FREES YOU FROM IDEOLOGY

"The world is always close to catastrophe. But it seems to be closer now. Seeing this approaching catastrophe, most of us take shelter in idea. We think that this catastrophe, this crisis, can be solved by an ideology. Ideology is always an impediment to direct relationship, which prevents action."

■ **JIDDU KRISHNAMURTI** ■
THE BOOK OF LIFE

Action immediately frees you from your ideologies. The switch is one of impossible (and invisible) reconciliation of warring ideas to total harmony. Focusing on the work or situation before you as it is makes it clear.

The most obvious choice becomes clear as you pay attention. When you let go of an idea of how things *should* be then you open yourself up to the best current choice.

This is easy to perform in work or sports, provided we have some experience with them.

It's more difficult in relationships with other people.

Our expectations for how our parents, significant others, or bosses *should* behave makes us blind to how we could act given the current circumstances. We shouldn't apply romantic ideals to others if we wish to connect with them. (Even the expectation that *they lift their expectations* should be lifted.)

CREATE CULTURE

> *"We have to create culture, don't watch TV, don't read magazines, don't even listen to NPR. Create your own roadshow. The nexus of space and time where you are now is the most immediate sector of your universe, and if you're worrying about Michael Jackson or Bill Clinton or somebody else, then you are disempowered, you're giving it all away to icons, icons which are maintained by an electronic media so that you want to dress like X or have lips like Y. This is shit-brained, this kind of thinking."*
>
> ◼ **TERRENCE MCKENNA** ◼

We often look at culture as something that we need to figure out so that we might fit into it or take advantage of it in some way. This is exhausting and ultimately futile.

Instead of assuming the posture that we must conform to a culture outside of us, we can instead decide to embody a culture of our own creation. Every action we take defines our personal culture and ripples outward.

The more you focus on taking bold actions the more other people will feel that they too can be bold.

The fact that you don't know about Justin Bieber spreads the idea that his every move isn't necessary information to participate in society.

Bohemianism has enabled groups of people with unpopular ideals to thrive for centuries. You, too, can choose to reject (or better, ignore) certain rules society has placed before you. Some come at little or no cost or change in your personal lifestyle (eating breakfast foods at dinnertime). Others are much easier to achieve when you join together with a group of people (it's easier to avoid capitalism when you're living on a commune than in Manhattan).

"That is all cultural diversion, and what is real is you and your friends and your associations, your highs, your orgasms, your hopes, your plans, your fears. And we are told 'no,' we're unimportant, we're peripheral. 'Get a degree, get a job, get a this, get a that.' And then you're a player, you don't want to even play in that game. You want to reclaim your mind and get it out of the hands of the cultural engineers who want to turn you into a half-baked moron consuming all this trash that's being manufactured out of the bones of a dying world."

■ **TERRENCE MCKENNA** ■

SELLING TILES

I have a friend who got a job selling tile out of college. He was scared. I talked with him the first day he started.

"It was nerve-racking going into a store where I wasn't wanted," he told me.

Two weeks later we spoke on the phone. He still hadn't made any sales, which was demoralizing, yet he had started to get more comfortable going in to stores to pitch them.

Six weeks later he had sold a ton of tile and was having fun refining his pitch. It became a game.

I asked him what he was doing that was different.

"I don't know, nothing really. I've just been doing it a while I guess."

How many times have you heard this story? You've probably experienced it before.

The first kiss is terrifying, the second is fun. Nobody makes varsity without experience playing first. Nobody writes well without writing badly first (in fact, most writers will tell you nobody writes well—editing just makes it look that way).

Repetitive action not only makes you better, it also makes it easier to begin again tomorrow.

DEEPER KNOWING

"There is more wisdom in your body than your deepest philosophy."

■ **FRIEDRICH NIETZSCHE** ■
THUS SPAKE ZARATHUSTRA

Do not be concerned about defining your philosophy or beliefs to others. An obsession with explanation will often trick us into thinking we are taking action—when we are just finding a more clever way to stagnate.

Remember Nassim Taleb's words, "...it is much better to do things you cannot explain than explain things you cannot do."

There is a deeper level of knowing within your body (beneath your conscious mind) than you will ever be able to explain.

A scientific study may find something about increasing creative potential, yet it may have no effect on you. You may not react to things the same way as the majority of their subjects. Remember that few studies find anything that affects 100% of people the same.

Trust your own experience—even the one you can't see clearly. There's constantly an n=1 experiment being run deep down in your bones.

FORGET HARM

> *"Choose not to be harmed—and you won't feel harmed.*
> *Don't feel harmed—and you haven't been."*
>
> ■ **MARCUS AURELIUS,** *MEDITATIONS* ■

Action forgets to be harmed.

TRAIN FOR COOLNESS

Voltaire told the First Duke of Marlborough that the secret to military success is "tranquil courage in the midst of tumult and serenity of soul in danger, which the English call a cool head."

The best way to a cool head? Exposure through action.

Training is the accumulation of actions we've taken to prepare for an event. It ups our skill level and creates a familiarity with an experience.

In the heat of a crisis, you know exactly how to act because you've acted that way many times before.

This is the origin of a common saying in the military: "You don't rise to the occasion, you sink to your level of training."

ACTION REPELS STRESS

Before going into battle, soldiers check their equipment repeatedly. This is important for safety; even more than that, it calms nerves through repetitive action.

Before a job interview, the rituals of shaving, ironing your shirt, and shining your shoes center your mind in preparation for a different kind of engagement.

Stress is like a mosquito; as soon as you stop moving, it finds you. Feasts on you.

Whenever you sit idly, stressful thoughts arrive in swarms.

Action acts as a repellent against such anxieties, keeping these bloodsuckers at bay.

ACTION BUILDS TOLERANCE FOR FAILURES

Focusing on taking action shifts the focus from failure to what was learned by the failure.

Failure still sucks. We still mourn our loss.

But we care more about correcting course.

ACTION SEIZES

> *"The best men are not those who have waited for chances but who have taken them; besieged chance, conquered the chance, and made chance the servitor."*
>
> ◼ **E. H. CHAPIN** ◼

The most powerful opportunities come when there seem to be none. When everyone else has thrown their hands up in despair you remain focused on taking action. You see the opportunities because you are engaged in reality—instead of a sad perception (abstraction!) of it.

Warren Buffet loves (from a business perspective) when the stock market crashes because it gives him an opportunity to get stocks cheap.

Many great companies were started in recessions or depressions.

The more tired you become the more tired your competition is. Every day you go back to work your competitors will drop off. The farther you push the less competition exists.

BAD QUESTIONS

There are certain questions that can only be overcome by action.

Am I happy?

As soon as it is asked, happiness disappears. It returns soon after it is forgotten.

What is my purpose in life?

This is only honestly answerable for a few people. There is no answer from God or the cosmos. Either you have to settle on something that comes from you (which I think you probably don't believe all the way) or you need to give the question up. It took a long time to admit it, but I finally found that life is much more about action than purpose. Execution of abstraction matters a lot.

Do I love this person?

As soon as you ask it you've fallen out of love. Love may be the least comprehensible thing in existence. (A biological explanation is no explanation that matters for living.)

Why live?

Because you're already breathing. Because you can take action. Of course, the real answer lies beyond the "because"; it's *in* the action you take now, next, forever.

Applying logic to bad questions is a formula for frustration, stagnation, and deep existential angst. Avoiding these are only possible through right action.

ACTION MAKES WASTING TIME IMPOSSIBLE

When you participate in right action there is absolutely no way you could be wasting time. You're making progress, you're learning, you're aware of emerging possibilities.

ACTION REVEALS THE REAL DREAM

There's a difference between wanting something and liking it. Sometimes we end up liking the things we want. Sometimes we want things we won't actually like.

Most of the things that sound amazing in the abstract are actually immensely tedious. Filmmaking, painting, and other "dream careers" have been romanticized to the point where we have been meant to feel guilty if we *don't* wish them for ourselves.

Our imaginations tell us fairytales about these lives. About the fame, the wealth, the happiness.

They might lead to a happily ever after for you. You might find the tedium and downsides are worth the satisfaction. You also might find that they're not at all as dreamy as you imagined.

There's only one way to find out: trying "fantasy" careers and other options for yourself. Not reading about them in books. Experiencing them in practice.

Taking action is freeing yourself from fairytales and connecting to reality. To the actual process of getting somewhere. Maybe you'll like what you want. Maybe your dream is your real dream...you won't know until you move towards it.

ACTION DEFIES "WHY?"

When embarking on any journey, the hero is bound to be asked, "Why?" by those being left behind.

Sometimes there is a perfectly good answer. Sometimes there isn't. And sometimes there shouldn't be.

The world begs you to justify yourself. *You* beg you to justify yourself. To explain exactly why you do what you do. They demand a story that makes sense.

Sometimes there isn't one. At least not one you can put into words.

The only real story is in your actions.

They may seem random at first. Like they don't make sense. After a while, though, they will.

After a while they will be clear enough. They will carry an explanation beyond anything you could make up.

ACTION STRIPS AWAY UNHELPFUL COMPARISONS

It is only in the midst of dedicated action that we lose our ability to compare ourselves to another. There is no better training for self-reliance than action. It takes all of our attention and puts it to use.

On the other hand, it is nearly impossible *not* to compare ourselves to others in abstraction. You set goals based on the goals of others. You set expectations based on the expectations of others. You decide your worth based on others.

Competition can certainly get us moving. The danger is in competing with someone running a different race. Or someone who's way too far ahead. In the first case, you'll get focused on the wrong things; in the second you'll get demoralized and lose your motivation.

Action frees you from these dangers. Then, eventually, it makes you invincible to them.

ACTION EMBRACES AMOR FATI

> *"My formula for greatness in a human being is amor fati: that one wants nothing to be different, not forward, not backward, not in all eternity. Not merely bear what is necessary, still less conceal it...but love it."*
>
> ◼ **FRIEDRICH NIETZSCHE,** *ECCE HOMO* ◼

Everything is used up—the good and the bad alike. Everything is transformed or amplified for the good of life. Everything in our history helps push us. Every weakness creates our strengths.

Everything we *must* do we now *get* to do.

Everything that happens is meant to happen. Not because it was ordained but because it *did* happen.

And whatever happens must be used.

"SUCKERS TRY TO WIN ARGUMENTS, NON-SUCKERS TRY TO WIN."
—NASSIM TALEB

Action is about the ultimate win—it transcends argument. Argument is derived from (and therefore secondary to) actions and their consequences.

Action immediately removes you from the squabble. It separates you from those afraid to make a move.

You cannot take action and remain petty, immaterial, or inane.

Action doesn't pretend to have an answer for everything—but it does accept that it may be the answer.

PART VI: SHAPING ACTIONS

"Be great in act, as you have been in thought—suit the action to the word, and the word to the action."

■ SHAKESPEARE ■

WHAT IS USEFUL?

Ruminating, or getting back to work?

Thinking about her saying *no,* or finding out if she will say *yes?*

Considering the lives you could have lived, or taking stock of what is available to you in this life?

Researching nutrition, or cutting sugar out of your diet?

Wishing your partner would be different, or giving them love for who they are?

Reading a list about what successful people do, or taking the first step on the project you've been putting off?

The work is more useful every time. The work required to love, to create, to live.

FORCE FUTURE ACTION

Demosthenes, the great Greek orator, holed up in a dugout he built in order to educate himself. He shaved half his head so that he would be too embarrassed to go outside. He shaped his environment to force right action in the future.

Look around. What can you do today that will force desired behavior tomorrow?

Demosthenes was asked—after he had become famous for his speeches—what the most important traits of speech-making were. He summed it up in three words, "Action, action, action!"

PROCESS

Nick Saban, the head coach of the University of Alabama football team, keeps his team focused on the process:

> *"Don't think about winning the SEC Championship. Don't think about the national championship. Think about what you need to do in this drill, on this play, in this moment. That's the process: Let's think about what we can do today, the task at hand."*

The step in front of you is the most important thing in the world. When you get to the big game, then that will be the most important thing in the world.

Your biggest opportunity is always right now.

SIMPLICITY

We opened this book with the following quote, it's worth re-visiting:

> *"The cucumber is bitter? Then throw it out. There are brambles in the path? Then go around. That's all you need to know."*
>
> ◼ **MARCUS AURELIUS** ◼

Problem. Action. Problem. Action.

Poke and prod. Find a way.

Action simplifies the process while dealing with complex problems. Action allows improvisation.

POST-FLINCH PUSH

> *"When jarred, unavoidably, by circumstances revert at once to yourself and don't lose the rhythm more than you can help. You'll have a better grasp of harmony if you keep going back to it."*
>
> ◼ **MARCUS AURELIUS** ◼

Unbroken, continuous right action is impossible. Unpleasant (and pleasant) surprises are one of the few things guaranteed in this life.

A surprise causes us to flinch away. To take a step back and second-guess ourselves.

We can't be in a perfect flow all the time. The idea is to shrink our time spent with inaction and maximize the time we spend taking action.

It's not all or nothing. It's incremental.

It's practice.

Don't fear the flinch—use it as a trigger. Train yourself to lean *into* the flinch.

All it takes is awareness and the willingness to be uncomfortable for a second.

You aren't going to die.

HOW TO DETERMINE RIGHT ACTION

Two rules:

- ■ Stop considering whether you *should.*
- ■ Stop considering if you are *ready.*

IT GETS HARDER AND EASIER

Action pushes you higher.

The problems you face don't get smaller.

They get bigger. Much bigger.

That's the bad news.

The good news?

You're more capable. You've proven your mettle.

The dragon is bigger because you are stronger.

ACTION WILL BE YOUR LEGACY

> *"He who has a vehement desire for posthumous fame does not consider that every one of those who remember him will himself also die very soon..."*
>
> ■ **MARCUS AURELIUS** ■

We can't escape the fact that we wish to leave the world with a reminder that we were here, too, once.

On some level it doesn't make much sense—the mind that is wishing to be remembered will probably be gone...it won't even have a chance to think about being remembered!

Some people can afford to put their name on football stadiums or tall buildings. Some people have left large tombs. Some have left autobiographies. Some have left massive fortunes. Some have left scientific breakthroughs.

Some glorious son-of-a-gun out there left us the PB&J sandwich.

These are great contributions. However, the accumulation of interactions you have with other people will certainly be greater.

The way you are in the world matters more than what you make in the world.

This is important.

You spread whatever you are. If you are decisive, emotionally stable, and optimistic, then you will give others the permission to be the same.

When you free yourself from overthinking and commit to action you will free others. Not by spreading the word or talking about this book (although that would be great!) but by just *being* that way.

Think of a time when you've been afraid to make a leap. You look around for others who have made the leap. Then you see it's a possibility.

When you smile at someone instead of worrying about what they're thinking about you, you make their day better—and your day better.

When you do the thing you're embarrassed to do you provide relief for everyone around who was too scared.

When you believe the actions you take are more important than an abstract purpose, you may pull an onlooker out of an existential crisis with you.

If you can do it, they can too. These moments multiply.

The person you smiled at while waiting in line at the grocery store was planning on committing suicide later that day. Now they are second-guessing it. They may continue to live and provide good for others, who will then provide more good for others.

Staying calm in the midst of an emergency will give solace to others. Now others will gain solace from them.

It's been called the butterfly effect.

We, as humans, are terrible at believing what isn't right in front of us. We sometimes feel like we're doing nothing, like our lives don't matter.

This is impossible.

If you think you can't create any change, then you will create change by spreading the idea of hopelessness.

Everything you do matters.

Act accordingly.

"Act well at the moment, and you have performed a good action for all eternity."

◼ **JOHANN KASPAR LAVATER** ◼

ABOUT THE AUTHOR

Kyle Eschenroeder is a writer who has been an entrepreneur, day trader, and whatever else sounded good at the time. Tweet at him @kyleschen.

If you want to kickstart your action habit, Kyle has created a course for you at TheActionCourse.com.